NOOK

CW01432243

Jasmine Williams

BookLeaf
Publishing

India | USA | UK

NOOK © 2023 Jasmine Williams

Presentation by *BookLeaf Publishing*

Web: www.bookleafpub.com

E-mail: info@bookleafpub.com

ISBN: 9789358313475

First edition 2023

DEDICATION

For Mum, Dad & Luke

As the firstborn and sibling, it's only right that my first book is for you - at the root of everything your qualities inspire me the most.

ACKNOWLEDGEMENT

My world has been inspired and impacted by my incredible family and all of the wonderous strangers, some of those becoming my friends for life, for which I am forever grateful.

Shuqi, thank you for being my oldest friend and proving true friendship can survive distance and time, you are the meaning of grace and an exemplary human being. Cathryn, thank you for teaching me how to be honest and open without fear, and for your introduction to classical music - I adore watching you perform and find it the most inspiring. Capucine my soul sister, this book wouldn't exist if you hadn't kept me grounded during lockdown with your magnificence and humour, I owe you my sanity, thank you. Special thanks to Leo for believing in my capacity to write and building up my confidence to host and perform for the very first time at your impactful poetry live night, you've taught me courage to the highest degree. Rachel A your poetry is remarkable and it inspires me to write, as does the belly laughter that afflicts me whenever I see you. Rachel H, thank you for being a shoulder to cry on and showing me what a home feels like in a strange place, not to mention for being an example of what an intelligent, powerful woman can do. I have never met someone so fearless, Mary you're the true meaning of going with the flow and I admire it. Uncle Danny, the teacher, and one of the first people to see me for who I am, I appreciate you. To the duo, now trio, of Question Life, the world seems a bigger place thanks to your shared knowledge and generosity, thank you. Tina your depth is captivating, as are your words. Ilaria & Cerys, your creativity is abundant and contagious, as are your good vibes! Adam, you are charm personified and everything I wished to find in a person, thank you always for embracing my ramblings on a day-to-day basis, I love you.

I wish I could mention everyone but I'd be here forever and a day, I can only hope you all know how important and valued you are!

Where I'm Coming From

The streets: my streets- and by that I mean
The brick maze where I was born and raised
Where my knees were grazed and eyes unseen,
From my bedroom window longingly gazed
At the clouds, mere shadows in the night sky

From up above it may not look colourful or soft
I don't believe if I jumped from this high
The buildings beneath would keep me aloft
Or even welcome me back in, but it deceives
Have you seen the cracks in the concrete smile?

Inside this city, I've never seen such vibrance
In the graffiti-adorned walls and the passion
Which laces it all together- locals and migrants
Working as one, an ethos constantly refashioned
To navigate the division in the depths of the
mind

These are mine, I'm curious to know your streets
To follow their map on the lines of your palms
Like a psalm hear the sky as you see it, peace

Arises with listening and understanding, not arms
I live for the day all streets converse in the language of unity

Lions Only Need Dens Outside of Nirvana

London
Where the river tames my adventurous heart
In the land of supposed opportunity
It's for the art, I'm trying to let that sink in
Without sinking into debt and the state that I'm
in
Go with the flow they always say
Shallowly hoping it's enough
To not drown or float away

London
Where the underground crawls into my lungs
The most connected city in the UK
Apparently, I should be lucky to be here
With so many people near, but I'm lonely
anyway
Rumbling and grumbling to work
To make it to the next payday

London
Where forced ignorance is a tumour
While blades poke holes in pockets and hearts

Don't go here or there alone
And make sure you've got your phone
But put it away so it's not grabbed
And don't speak up and don't look mad
And for the love of God, don't get stabbed

London
Where if it's a mixed bag you want you've got it
The world sees so many awful things
But it's raw and exciting from time to time
I've found new souls and they've found mine
A foraged community of the lost and found
So that despite it all
I'll stick around

Two Trains in Time

I visited a parallel universe today
And I didn't even have to leave my seat
I was on the train in the pouring rain
With disgustingly soaking feet

My playlist became dramatic
So I gazed out of the window to play along of
course
And then I locked eyes with myself in disguise
But they didn't blink back at the source!

I thought, that's it I've finally lost it
Go ahead and deliver me to the looney bin
Then the train moved away, scene like a Monet
As the raindrops melted her skin

Raindrop to raindrop, train to train
Impatience on parallel tracks too explicit
Divergent lives lived in vain
Bought together anyway, for less than a minute

No Return

Irony is a landfill filling me with emptiness
As birds, like debris, circle forgotten remnants
Looking for what they do not know to find
Akin to us searching for purpose
In this oblivion we are consigned

Crane-ium

While bodies were squirming under the flames
My mind was trying to remember the names
For the long metal limb from which the moon
Dangled from three ropes, swaying to the tune
Of hysterical high laughter and blood bursting
bass
Under the majestic crane with an eye on its face
With mine tilted up with a vacant gaze
Fond images apparate from beneath the haze
In the present, memories recline in my mind
I remember finding everything I had hoped to
find
Melting the cobwebs, capturing happiness
within
All I had the pleasure of meeting, the people we
had been
That night is one of the best I've known
Signalling the emergence from the Dead Zone

Sticky Buds in Summer

You and I were so inseparable
The way sticky buds in summer
Clung to our jumpers
To remove would render them irreparable
Just as we would be without each other

Stuck on so fast they're still
Hitching a ride to the classroom
Laughter behind turned backs
As you come to a standstill
Watching confusion bloom

Ignorant to a return attack
Laughing away until the next day
"You've ruined my washing again?!"
Followed by a hearty whack
The cycle resumes there and then

The light of fond memories is hazy
Reality so far from that image
But I'll never forget those days with you
And sometimes I miss you like crazy
Even though, as I watched, the distance grew
Like those sticky buds in summer

The Observed Observes, Absurd

The mist of time fogs my brain
Loose hands spurning dashing rain
To think takes more than I can give
But without thought I cannot live

In this house of frames I hoped to find
An otherness to soothe my mind
A pause, a breath, a reason to be
Something exquisite, much more than me

An elephantine landscape to outrun time
A voyage to make the setting sun mine
Bright green pastures and dotted lakes
Scribbles, intentional and without mistake

The Ugly Duchess questions beauty and style
For what is forgotten, makes others smile
The mist of time settles as glistening dew
Bringing clarity, hope and vitality anew

Penmanship

There are fewer things more beautiful
Than the loops and lines of ink
As they run from your fingertips
Across the page, begging to be chased
By my hungry eyes
Each letter, every word dancing
Across my irises, joining
The party around the fire of my imagination
As we hold hands and move to the
Flames and the music
Which follows an erratic beat
Such as the way you dot your 'i's
Or cross your 't's
One which quickens my heart
And buries my thoughts under the
River of black which pleasantly resides
On the rough white pages
That sleep under my bed
Until I am ready to read them again

Tunnelling

I could quantum tunnel right into you
And as sure as the light from the sun
We would create an energy so strong
Even the night wouldn't stop the clouds
Being visible in the sky

Benches

So many remnants of wandering thoughts
So many ideas, an equal amount of naughts
Barrels of tears and lone wooden smiles
Of those who have sat here a good long while

Never seen to move but always alive
Words and entanglements, an emotional hive
Nobody thinks of a simple bench standing
Who's there for us all, from cloud nine to crash
landing

Black Holes in Conversation

Silence is not uncomfortable at all
Just admire the leaves of the thoughts that fall
Reach out and ruffle them with your mind alone
The feathers that are not intentionally shown
Be tickled with delight at the knowledge that
springs
More powerful than all the world's queens and
kings
Silence will lead you where words will not
follow
So listen for it today, lest it evade you tomorrow

Lighthouses With Legs

Candy canes against heavy grey
Beacons for heads to light the way
Lighthouses with legs led astray
Into the thunder they go

The wailing rain threatens to pound
The bullying clouds from sky to ground
The searching beams slice the sound
Better the devil you know

Waves snap and bite at bony shins
Like tiny dogs with salty chins
Despite the light they step right in
Into the blackness below

A second as the surface becomes aglow
With all they've seen and all they know
Drawn to the danger of what they show
And what we should have seen

STEM

Repetition is something of a haunting melody
Sending staccato whispers down my brain stem
Sprouting through every pore accidentally
Unwavering anxiety, I need a pen
Inserted into my trachea to breathe again

I vomit flowers: an apology for what's to come
Sickly sweet truths of a contemplative heart
Contracted so tightly to crawl is to run
Across nails, I cannot move a foot apart
The ending is simpler than knowing where to
start

Sanctum

I wish to be wrapped in those patchwork fields,
Miles upon miles of fragrant hills
The hum of the ground's creatures my lullaby
Fuelling the earth I would be, should I cry
For it would not soak the cotton beneath my chin
To last until the morning sun rises therein

My limbs could wind through grass and wheat
Without worry of kicking window plants with
my feet
Lungs blooming in the presence of hope and
fresh air
Not stifled by silence and helpless despair
For my space is my own, under my grassy quilt
Where my peace is strong and will not again wilt

Questions Unanswered

A child once asked me, ever so politely
Why do bad things happen to good people
nightly?
Then he bowed his head ever so contritely
And I tilted his chin up ever so slightly
Sympathised with the pain in his eyes of what
might be
I might have squeezed his hand a little too
tightly
And said, yet in a sky full of terrors, how does
the eagle still fly
Through the sky
So mightily?

Mutation of Matter

I pluck the strings
And they twang and quiver
I play you my song
You cry me a river

I tighten them up
To create more tension
The notes are higher
A stairway to heaven

I tighten them more
They snap and break
You sit in silence
Your breath to take

No more strings
So I'll use my keys
To satisfy and quench
Your stormy seas

When life gives you nothing
When it likes to sit and tease
Turn thoughts into strings
And strings into keys

Never Truly Touched

Penetration used to feel like we were fully
touching
But now I know it's just our electrons pushing
against each other
My atoms have never felt your atoms
A kiss that feels so pleasing
Fingers trailing over my skin leaving
goosebumps
Intimacy is all in the mind
We've never truly touched
But I can feel your energy
And something about that feels really good
Like we can still be connected, a human's tool
That even if it's in the empty space
That empty space is the most comforting of all

Earth's Balm

If birds and bees could whisper, talk
Sweet honey would give you flight
Forget perdition and puddled stalk
To love is a human right

Chopstick Confidence

I want the kind of confidence that
Is unwavering, un-shaking
Walk into any room un-quaking
Despite the chopsticks I'm taking

Wooden, metal, plastic
None of them would defeat me
And I'd devour the meal so completely
A total success, I could guarantee

No morsel would escape
No dribble down my chin
Not a single twitch in my grin
No tiny violin

I would remain triumphant
Nothing in my voice would betray
Any worries or dismay
Even if my mind was in disarray

I want that kind of confidence
That comes with using chopsticks for years
The type that doesn't end in tears
Or turn them into spears

Out of pure desperation

Yeah

I want that chopstick kind of confidence

Fake Trackies & Ripped CD's

Inside the market stalls
Around which fabric drapes soft walls
Mum puts back what we can't afford
Just to point you both toward
A table full of ripped CDs for the taking
Soul and R&B, as you're a singer in the making
Machinations of world domination begin
Itinerant notions that follow you like kin
Niggling little brother at your side
Enigmatic smile, dragging your arm, eyes wide
Wading through squashed chips on the ground
It's the latest pair of Jordans that he's found
Laughing at the mistakes abound
Leave that alone and get something simple
I say, at least they can't mess up a Nike Symbol
Around his neck, I drape a fake blue trackie
Man, it's like Christmas come early even if
nowadays it's tacky
Sadness ensues at how simple it was back then

Ghost of Me

Fire in your belly
Burns with mirth, longing, and laughter
Seek me there

Milton Keynes UK
Ingram Content Group UK Ltd.
UKHW050734170424
441314UK00014B/353